Incredible Plants!

What's That Plant?

Cody Crane

Children's Press®
An Imprint of Scholastic Inc.

Content Consultant
Michael Freeling, PhD
Professor
Department of Plant & Microbial Biology
University of California, Berkeley
Berkeley, California

Library of Congress Cataloging-in-Publication Data
Names: Crane, Cody, author.
Title: What's That Plant / by Cody Crane.
Description: New York, NY : Children's Press, an imprint of Scholastic Inc., 2020. | Series: A true book |
    Includes bibliographical references and index.
Identifiers: LCCN 2019004808 | ISBN 9780531234679 (library binding) | ISBN 9780531240106 (paperback)
Subjects: LCSH: Plants—Juvenile literature.
Classification: LCC QK49 .C83 2020 | DDC 581—dc23
LC record available at https://lccn.loc.gov/2019004808

All rights reserved. Published in 2020 by Children's Press, an imprint of Scholastic Inc.
Printed in Heshan, China 62

SCHOLASTIC, CHILDREN'S PRESS, A TRUE BOOK™, and associated logos are trademarks and/or registered trademarks of Scholastic Inc.
Scholastic Inc., 557 Broadway, New York, NY 10012
1 2 3 4 5 6 7 8 9 10 R 29 28 27 26 25 24 23 22 21 20

Front cover: Far left, baobab; top middle, king proteas; top right, organ pipe cactus; center, fern with spores; middle right, liverwort; bottom middle, sunflowers; bottom right, mangrove

Back cover: Bristlecone pine

Find the Truth!

Everything you are about to read is true *except* for one of the sentences on this page.

Which one is **TRUE**?

T or F Only some plants produce flowers.

T or F Seaweed is a type of plant.

Find the answers in this book.

3

Contents

The BIG Truth

Is It a Plant?

Tulips

The leaves of some trees change color in fall.

The inside of a flower

Think About It!

What do you see in this image? To figure it out, examine the photo closely. What details jump out at you right away? Now look again. Are there any details you missed before? What do you already know about plants that can help you describe what you see? Give evidence to support your claim.

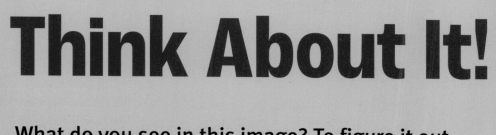

Intrigued?
Want to know more? Turn the page!

Rainbow eucalyptus can grow to be more than 25 stories tall!

If you guessed that this is a tree trunk, then you are right! You might have figured out that you were looking at a tree. But why does its trunk have so many colors? This tree is a rainbow eucalyptus. It grows in tropical forests in Indonesia, Papua New Guinea, and the Philippines. The tree has thin bark that peels away in strips. The tissue beneath looks bright green at first because it contains **chlorophyll**. All plants have this green pigment, or coloring, to harness the sun's energy to make food.

After the rainbow eucalyptus loses a strip of bark, chlorophyll in the exposed area begins to break down. Its green color fades. Other purple, orange, and red pigments start to build up. The result: a tree with rainbow-colored stripes!

This tree is just one of the amazing plants found on our planet. This book will help you discover and classify them into different types.

Plants come in many shapes and sizes.

The cottony fluff on Arctic cotton grass was traditionally used to make candle wicks.

Arctic cotton grass thrives in the cold wetlands of the north.

The Plant Kingdom

Plants come in all shapes and sizes. They range from huge water lilies to tiny dandelions. In fact, more than 390,000 plant **species** exist on Earth. Together, they make up the plant kingdom.

You can find plants on every continent. They live in all types of environments. The frozen Arctic? Surprise! Plants live there. The Sahara Desert in Africa? Yep! You will find plants there, too. Plants are everywhere!

This is a fossil of a *Cooksonia*, a very early land plant found in what is now England.

The First Plants

Picture Earth without plants. Bare rock covers the ground. No trees. No flowers. No grass. That is what it was like before plants first appeared hundreds of millions of years ago!

Early plants were different from most modern plants. They had no true leaves, roots, or stems. We know how these plants looked because of **fossils**. Some ancient plants left impressions in mud. The mud hardened over time into rock. That preserved the imprint of the plant as a fossil.

The Kingdoms of Life

Scientists divide the estimated 8.7 million species on Earth into six kingdoms. Every creature, from roses to frogs to mushrooms, falls into one of these groups.

ANIMALIA
Animals must eat other organisms to survive. This kingdom includes all animals.

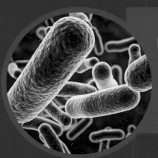

PLANTAE
Nearly all plants make their own food. They provide other organisms with food, oxygen, shelter, and other materials.

FUNGI
Fungi break down decaying matter and absorb its nutrients to live. Fungi can be one **cell** or many cells.

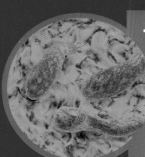

EUBACTERIA
Eubacteria are made up of just one cell. Only a few are germs that cause disease.

PROTISTA
Some protista are similar to plants. Others are more like animals or fungi. Most are single-celled. Some live in colonies.

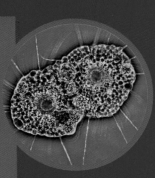

ARCHAEBACTERIA
Despite the name, archaebacteria are not really bacteria. These single-celled organisms live in the most extreme places on Earth.

Plant Ancestors

Have you seen what looks like green scum floating in a pond? That gunk is **algae**. Scientists think ancient algae-like organisms gave rise to modern plants. Today, broad definitions of "plant" can include algae, but algae are generally labeled protists. Almost all algae live in water. Some are just one cell. Others contain many cells and can look similar to plants. Like plants, algae use chlorophyll to harness light to make food.

Green algae can grow fast, covering lakes, rivers, and oceans in thick slime.

Branching Out

Plants quickly spread. They developed new traits, such as leaves and roots. These characteristics affected how plants looked and functioned. New species arose, each with a unique set of features. Plants passed these traits on as they reproduced. And the traits continued to change. Some changes resulted in species that have since gone extinct. Others continued to produce new generations for millions of years, developing into the plant world we see today.

Nearly all cactus species are native to North and South America.

Saguaro, the largest cacti in the United States, can grow up to 50 feet (15 m) tall.

Mangroves help protect coastal land from wind and water damage during storms.

Many marine animals make their home among mangrove roots.

Home Sweet Home

Plants develop traits that help them survive in different habitats. Cacti, for example, have adapted to store water in their stems. That allows them to live in places that are extremely hot and dry. Mangrove trees, on the other hand, live where it is really wet. They grow along shores. The trees have developed long roots to anchor themselves in the water.

Energy from the Sun

Nearly all plants on Earth share one important trait: They harness the sun's rays to make food. This process is called **photosynthesis**. It happens inside plants' leaves. They take in water and carbon dioxide gas from the air. Then chlorophyll helps turn these substances into sugar that plants use for energy. Plants give off oxygen as waste during photosynthesis. Other living things, including people, need this oxygen to breathe. They can also use plants for food.

Mature sunflowers face east to catch the strong rays of the morning sun.

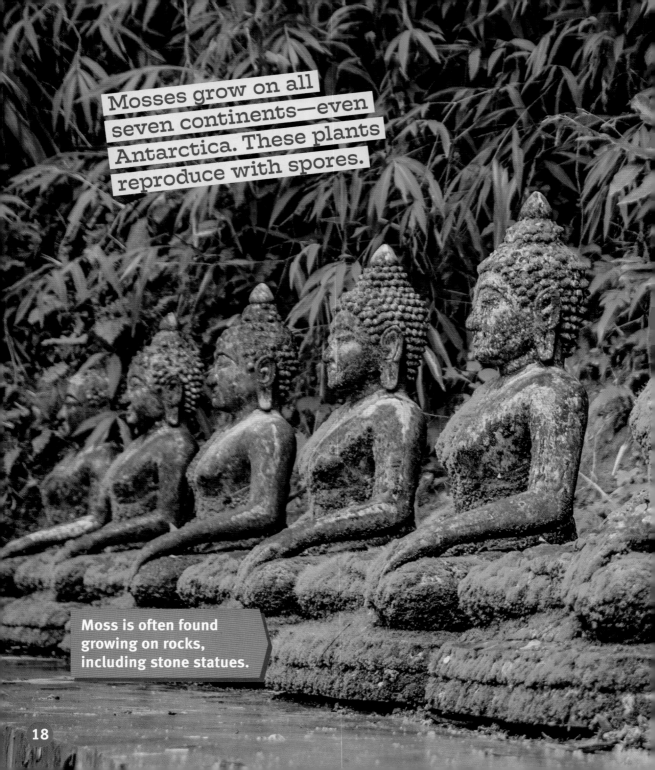

Mosses grow on all seven continents—even Antarctica. These plants reproduce with spores.

Moss is often found growing on rocks, including stone statues.

Seedless Plants

Different plant species can often seem nothing alike. But they can be divided into groups that share basic traits. One way to do this is by looking at how the plants reproduce, or make offspring. Some plants use flowers to produce seeds. They're the planet's newest type of plant. Plants that use cones to produce seeds are older. Other plants reproduce with **spores**. They are the most ancient of all.

Mosses and Liverworts

Mosses and liverworts are among the oldest plant types seen today. They lack a **vascular system**. Instead of tubes carrying nutrients through their bodies, these plants absorb water from the air.

Mosses look like fuzzy, green carpet. They often cover forest floors, logs, and rocks. Liverworts are patches of small, flat, leafy or leaf-like plants that grow close to the ground. Both plants have short hairs, instead of roots, that anchor them to surfaces.

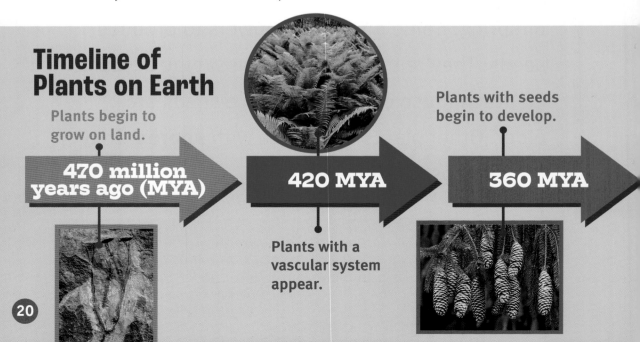

Timeline of Plants on Earth

Plants begin to grow on land.

470 million years ago (MYA)

420 MYA

Plants with a vascular system appear.

Plants with seeds begin to develop.

360 MYA

Ferns and Horsetails

Except for extinct plants, ferns and horsetails were the first nonflowering plants to develop a vascular system. That allowed them to grow larger than other nonflowering plants. Some grow as tall as trees.

Ferns grow leaves called fronds. These start out as tightly curled-up buds, which then unfurl. Horsetails look like tall stalks, sometimes with wispy leaves. Only a few horsetail species still exist. Most have gone extinct.

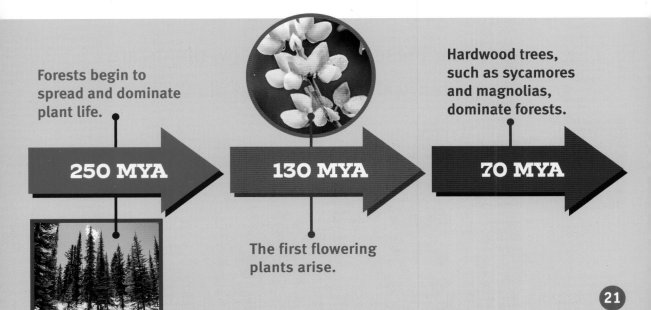

Forests begin to spread and dominate plant life.

250 MYA

Hardwood trees, such as sycamores and magnolias, dominate forests.

130 MYA

70 MYA

The first flowering plants arise.

Making New Plants

Sometimes to reproduce, mosses and liverworts make male and female cells. These combine to create spores. The spores grow inside capsules at the end of stalks. When the capsules dry out, they open to release the spores into the air. If they land somewhere damp, the spores **germinate** into a new plant.

All these plants, however, don't need spores to reproduce. Sometimes a part of the plant breaks apart or breaks off. Whole new plants can grow from these pieces. The new plants are genetically identical to the original plant.

Once a liverwort releases its spores, the wind carries the tiny particles to a new location.

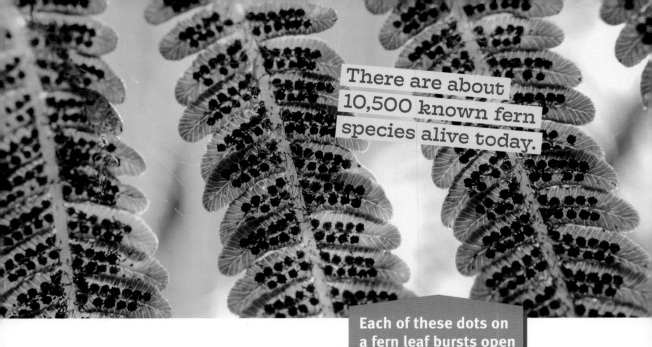

There are about 10,500 known fern species alive today.

Each of these dots on a fern leaf bursts open to release spores.

Two Stages

Ferns and horsetails also produce spores. They grow on the underside of fern fronds or in bunches at the tip of horsetail stalks. When released, these spores don't germinate into a fern or horsetail right away. First, they grow into a totally different plant shaped like a flat leaf. It makes male and female cells. They combine, and a spore-forming plant grows from the flat leaf. The new plant looks like the original fern or horsetail.

Is It a Plant?

Many living things look very similar to plants. But do not be fooled. Take a closer look at some common organisms that often get mistaken for members of the plant kingdom.

Mushrooms

Mushrooms grow out of the soil. But that is about all they have in common with plants. Mushrooms are in the fungi kingdom. They do not make their own food like plants. Instead, they eat decaying matter.

Kelp

Kelp, or seaweed, grows in vast forests in parts of the ocean. Kelp is green, and each one looks like it has a long stem with leaves. But it is actually a type of algae, which are generally considered protists.

Lichens

Lichens look a bit like moss. Both grow on rocks and trees. But lichens are not related to moss at all. They are actually things made up of either algae or bacteria living among fungi.

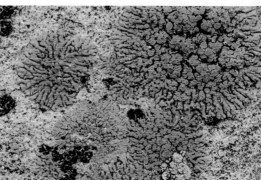

Corals

A coral is a tiny animal. Corals attach themselves to the ocean floor. Then they build a hard skeleton around themselves. Like plants, they stay rooted to this same spot for their whole lives.

Sea Anemones

Ocean creatures called sea anemones are named after a colorful flower found on land. But although they look like blossoms, they are not plants. Anemones are animals closely related to corals.

More than 90 percent of plants produce flowers.

Flowers come in every shade of color.

Flower Power

Flowering plants make up the largest group of plants on Earth. People have long been attracted to their blossoms. Many people grow them in gardens or give them in bouquets as gifts. Their fragrant petals become perfume. Flowers often look pretty and smell nice. But plants do not create them just for them to end up in a vase on a kitchen table. The job of all flowers is to help plants reproduce.

Purpose of Petals

Flowers can have male parts, female parts, or both. It just depends on the plant. The male parts produce pollen. This is a powdery, yellow substance. Pollen contains male cells. If pollen lands on the female part of a flower, male cells can join with female cells there. This is called **fertilization**. The combined cells develop into seeds. Each of these seeds can grow into a new plant.

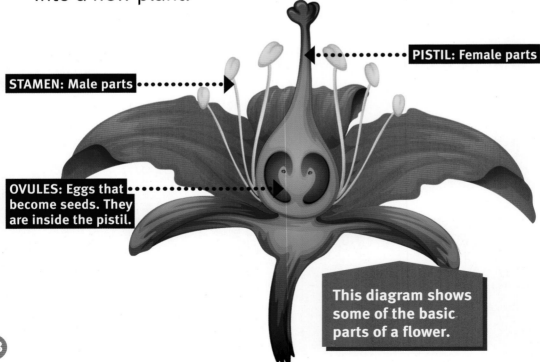

STAMEN: Male parts

PISTIL: Female parts

OVULES: Eggs that become seeds. They are inside the pistil.

This diagram shows some of the basic parts of a flower.

Clumps of pollen stick to hairs on bees' bodies.

Pollen Delivery

Some plants rely on the wind to spread pollen from flower to flower. But many plants get help from bees, butterflies, hummingbirds, and bats. These plants often have brightly colored, sweet-smelling flowers that attract the animals. The creatures visit the flowers to drink the sugary nectar inside. When they stop by for a sip, they often pick up some pollen by accident. They then leave some of this pollen on the next plant they visit, fertilizing it.

Creating Cones

Some trees produce flowers. They belong to the same plant group as other flowering plants (see page 34). Other trees are part of a separate plant group that produces seeds with cones instead of flowers. They include redwoods, pines, and cedars. These trees produce male cones, female cones, or both. Pollen from male cones travels by wind or insects to female cones to form seeds (see page 36).

Scattering Seeds

Once a plant forms seeds, it needs a way to spread them. Some seeds grow inside tasty fruit. Animals eat the fruit and scatter the seeds in their droppings. There are also prickly seeds, like burs, that stick to animals' fur. Other seeds are shaped so they can drift on the wind. A breeze can carry them far away. Still, other plants have pods that burst open, flinging seeds far and wide.

A dandelion seed can drift more than 5 miles (8 kilometers).

The common dandelion once grew only in Eurasia, but has spread across North America.

A baobab's trunk can store large amounts of water.

Baobab trees, like these in Africa, grow in drier parts of the world.

CHAPTER

4

Terrific Trees

What sets trees apart from other plants? Well, for one, they are a lot taller. Some tower over their surroundings. That allows them to soak up more sunlight. Unlike other plants, trees also have a woody stem called a trunk. Usually, a tree's trunk grows thicker as it grows taller. That helps support the tree's weight. Trees often grow together in forests. They can be found all over the world.

Deciduous Trees

Trees fall into two main groups: deciduous and evergreen. Deciduous trees have broad, flat leaves. They reproduce using flowers. They often produce nuts, such as acorns or pecans, instead of a typical fruit. A nut is a seed surrounded by a hard outer covering. Many deciduous trees grow in temperate areas. There, temperatures vary from season to season. But these trees can also be found in tropical areas where it is warm all year long.

Deciduous trees change throughout the seasons.

Leaves are bright green during the spring and summer.

Other pigments form for some trees, turning leaves red.

Chlorophyll breaks down, revealing new colors in the autumn.

Leaves dry up and turn brown, dropping from the tree by the end of fall.

Color Change

All deciduous trees lose their leaves during part of the year. This happens in autumn, when temperatures cool, or during dry seasons. It depends on where the trees grow. Their leaves often change color before they drop off. Chlorophyll, which normally makes leaves green, begins to break down. As it disappears, yellow and orange pigments once hidden by chlorophyll can be seen. Some tree leaves also make red pigments.

Evergreen Trees

Evergreen trees have leaves that remain green year-round. They do not shed their leaves all at once like deciduous trees do. Instead, evergreens lose and replace their leaves slowly throughout the year. Many evergreens are cone-producing plants called conifers. Conifers grow in cooler parts of the world. They have leaves shaped like sharp needles or flat scales.

Most pine trees live in northern areas.

The tallest trees in the world are evergreens. Some stand taller than the Statue of Liberty!

36

Palm trees are evergreens. They stay green year-round.

Other Evergreens

Not all evergreen trees live in chilly climates. You can even find them at the beach! Some evergreens, such as palm and coconut trees, live where it is hot. These tropical plants have tall trunks with a crown of leaves at the top that look like feathers. The leaves are usually pointy so rainwater can easily pour off of them. Other warm-weather evergreens, such as fig and eucalyptus trees, grow in tropical rain forests.

Bristlecone pines like this one can live thousands of years, surviving bad soil and damaging weather.

Ancient Forests

Trees can live longer than any other organism on Earth. The oldest living tree is a bristlecone pine in California's White Mountains. It's 5,062 years old! Ancient trees can be found in old-growth forests, where people have cut down very few of the trees. These forests can be hundreds or even thousands of years old. They are often home to some of the largest trees, which have been growing for a very long time.

Tree or Treelike?

Is bamboo a tree? Like many trees, bamboo flowers. Some types of bamboo are large, with hard, woody stems. And bamboo often grows in forests, like trees. But as treelike as bamboo seems, it is actually a grass!

Even so, this grass is amazing. It grows fast. One type of bamboo is actually the world's fastest growing plant! Plus, bamboo forests have a secret: Each stalk is actually part of the same plant! New shoots sprout from a part of the plant that is underground.

Bamboo stalks sprouting from the same parent plant is an example of vegetative reproduction.

How Old?

Each year, a new layer of wood is added around a tree's trunk and branches. These layers are called growth rings. You can learn how old a tree is by counting them. You can even tell how fast a tree grew each year by looking at the width of the rings. What do you think might cause a tree to grow faster or slower?

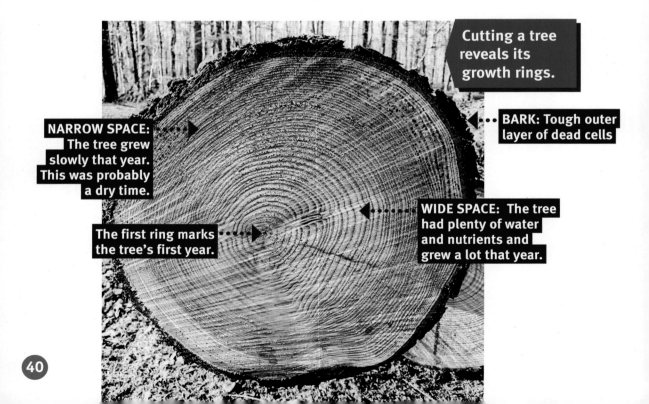

Cutting a tree reveals its growth rings.

NARROW SPACE: The tree grew slowly that year. This was probably a dry time.

BARK: Tough outer layer of dead cells

The first ring marks the tree's first year.

WIDE SPACE: The tree had plenty of water and nutrients and grew a lot that year.

The plants in the Amazon rain forest produce 20 percent of Earth's oxygen.

The Amazon rain forest is nicknamed the lungs of the world.

Important Organisms

There are many, many types of plants. That is a good thing for us—and the planet. All those different plants provide most of the food that animals eat. They produce cotton and other fibers we use to make clothes. We use them to create medicines. They supply wood for homes, furniture, and paper products. Plants also pump out oxygen for us to breathe. Nothing on Earth could survive without these amazing organisms!

Hidden Hues!

What causes leaves to change color?
Try this activity to learn more.

Materials

five green leaves
Scissors
Drinking glass
Wooden spoon
Rubbing alcohol
Measuring spoon
Paper towel

Directions

1 Use the scissors to cut the leaves into small pieces. Place the pieces in the glass. Pound them with the wooden spoon for five minutes.

2 Add a tablespoon of rubbing alcohol to the glass. Stir and let sit for 30 minutes. Then scoop out the leaf pieces.

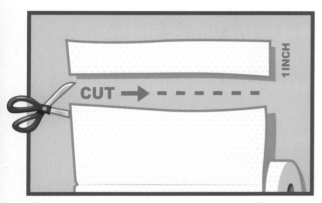

3 Cut a long strip 1 inch (2.5 centimeters) wide from the paper towel.

4 Dip one end of the strip into the liquid in the glass. Fold the other end of the strip over the rim of the glass.

5 Watch as the liquid moves up the strip. You will see separate bands of color. They are the different pigments that were in the leaves.

Explain It!

Using what you learned in the book, can you explain what happened with the leaves and why? If you need help, turn back to page 35 for more information.

True Statistics

Size of the Tongass National Forest in Alaska, the largest old-growth forest in the United States: 17 million acres (6.9 million ha)

Speed at which the fastest-growing plant—a kind of bamboo—can grow: 35 in. (89 cm) per day

Number of plant species on Earth that people can eat: 30,000

Number of plant species that supply about half of all plants people eat: 3 (corn, rice, and wheat)

Number of plant species used to make medicines: More than 50,000

Did you find the truth?

(T) Only some plants produce flowers.

(F) Seaweed is a type of plant.

Resources

Other books in this series:

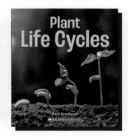

You can also look at:

Lawrence, Ellen. *Plants*. New York: Bearport Publishing, 2016.

Sohn, Emily, and Erin Ash Sullivan. *New Plants*. Chicago: Norwood Press, 2019.

Willis, K. J. *Botanicum*. Somerville, MA: BPP, 2017.

Glossary

algae (AL-jee) organisms made of one or many cells that usually live in water and contain chlorophyll

cell (SEL) the smallest unit of an animal, plant, or other organism

chlorophyll (KLOR-uh-fil) the green substance in plants that uses light to make food from carbon dioxide and water

fertilization (fur-tuh-luh-ZAY-shuhn) the process by which a male cell and a female cell join to reproduce an organism

fossils (FAH-suhlz) bones, shells, or other traces of an organism from millions of years ago, preserved as rock

germinate (JUR-muh-nate) to sprout, or put out shoots

photosynthesis (foh-toh-SIN-thuh-sus) a chemical process by which green plants and some other organisms make their food

species (SPEE-sheez) one of the groups into which animals, plants, and other organisms are divided; members of the same species can mate and produce offspring

spores (SPORZ) tiny particles used for reproduction that are made up of just a few cells protected by a tough coating

vascular system (VAS-cyoo-lur SIS-tuhm) the system of tubes that carry water and nutrients throughout an organism's body

Index

Page numbers in **bold** indicate illustrations.

About the Author

Cody Crane is an award-winning children's writer, specializing in nonfiction. She studied science and environmental journalism at New York University. Before becoming an author, she was set on becoming a biologist. She later discovered that writing about science could be just as fun as doing the real thing. She lives in Houston, Texas, with her husband and son.